BLAZERS

The U.S. Armed Forces

The U.S. Army Rangers

by Carrie A. Braulick

Consultant:
Barbara J. Fox
Reading Specialist
North Carolina State University

Capstone
press

Mankato, Minnesota

Blazers is published by Capstone Press,
151 Good Counsel Drive, P.O. Box 669, Mankato, Minnesota 56002.
www.capstonepress.com

Library of Congress Cataloging-in-Publication Data
Braulick, Carrie A., 1975–
    The U.S. Army Rangers / by Carrie A. Braulick.
    p. cm.—(Blazers. The U.S. Armed Forces)
    Summary: "Describes the U.S. Army Rangers, including their missions, vehicles, weapons, equipment, and duties"—Provided by publisher.
    Includes bibliographical references and index.
    ISBN 0-7368-4394-9 (hardcover)
    1. United States. Army—Commando troops—Juvenile literature. I. Title. II. Series.
UA34.R36B73 2006
356'.167'0973—dc22   2004028599

Credits
Juliette Peters, set designer; Patrick D. Dentinger, book designer; Jo Miller, photo researcher; Scott Thoms, photo editor

Photo Credits
Corbis, 6, 8, 14, 20, 21, 25; NewSport/George Tiedemann, 5, 28–29; Reuters, 11; Reuters/Philippines/Stringer, 18 (top)
DVIC/PH2 Kenneth J. Riley, USN, 18 (bottom)
Getty Images Inc./AFP/U.S. Army, 17; Erik S. Lesser, 22–23, 26, 27; Time Life Pictures/Mai/Mai, cover (inset)
U.S. Army Special Operations Command, 7; Nancy Fischer, 13; SSG Amanda C. Glenn, 15
The Viesti Collection Inc., cover

Capstone Press thanks Steve Maguire, president, U.S. Army Ranger Association, for his technical assistance in preparing this book.

1 2 3 4 5 6 10 09 08 07 06 05

Table of Contents

The Rangers in Action

Rangers jump out of a helicopter. Below them, enemy soldiers hide in an old building.

The Rangers reach the ground. They quietly surround the building. Suddenly, they break down the door.

The Rangers rush inside.
They capture the enemy
soldiers. Their mission is
a success.

BLAZER FACT

With just 18 hours of
notice, Rangers can be
almost anywhere in
the world.

Ranger Vehicles

The U.S. Army Rangers are highly trained soldiers. They often jump from aircraft. They open parachutes to land safely.

Ranger Special Operations Vehicles (RSOVs) help Rangers travel quickly. Rangers use them to take over airports.

Ranger Special Operations Vehicle (RSOV)

BLAZER FACT

The RSOV can be used
as a weapons carrier,
communications vehicle,
or medical vehicle.

Kawasaki KLR250 motorcycle

Rangers have motorcycles that easily travel over rough land. Helicopters sometimes bring the motorcycles to mission areas.

Weapons and Equipment

Rangers use many types of weapons. They carry some weapons. Other weapons are on top of vehicles.

M4 rifle

M249 Squad Automatic Weapon (SAW)

The lightweight M4 rifle is easy to carry. The M249 Squad Automatic Weapon (SAW) fires bullets quickly.

BLAZER FACT

Rangers sometimes put makeup on soldiers to make them appear to have wounds. They then practice treating the wounds.

The equipment Rangers use depends on their mission. They may use first aid supplies or communications equipment.

Ranger Equipment

M4 rifle

Binoculars

Squad radio earpiece

M136 AT4 antitank weapon

Canteen

Ranger Jobs

Rangers are trained for certain jobs. Some Rangers closely watch enemy soldiers. Snipers shoot at long-distance targets.

Rangers train hard for their jobs. Officers lead enlisted members during training. Strong, skilled soldiers are ready for even the toughest missions.

ARMY RANKS

ENLISTED
Private
Private First Class
Specialist
Sergeant

OFFICERS
Second Lieutenant
First Lieutenant
Captain
Major
Lieutenant Colonel
Colonel
General

A daring jump!

Glossary

airport (AIR-port)—a place where aircraft take off and land

bullet (BUL-it)—a small, pointed metal object fired from a gun

enlisted member (en-LISS-tuhd MEM-bur)—a member of the military who is not an officer

mission (MISH-uhn)—a military task

officer (OF-uh-sur)—a military member who directs enlisted members in their duties

parachute (PA-ruh-shoot)—a large piece of strong, lightweight fabric; parachutes allow people to jump from high places and float safely to the ground.

rifle (RYE-fuhl)—a powerful gun that is fired from the shoulder

sniper (SNY-pur)—a soldier trained to shoot at long-distance targets from a hidden place

target (TAR-git)—an object that is aimed at or shot at

Read More

Burgan, Michael. *U.S. Army Special Operations Forces: Airborne Rangers.* Warfare and Weapons. Mankato, Minn.: Capstone Press, 2000.

Green, Michael, and Gladys Green. *The U.S. Army Rangers at War.* On the Front Lines. Mankato, Minn.: Capstone Press, 2004.

Roberts, Jeremy. *U.S. Army Special Operations Forces.* U.S. Armed Forces. Minneapolis: Lerner, 2005.

Internet Sites

FactHound offers a safe, fun way to find Internet sites related to this book. All of the sites on FactHound have been researched by our staff.

Here's how:

1. Visit *www.facthound.com*
2. Type in this special code **0736843949** for age-appropriate sites. Or enter a search word related to this book for a more general search.
3. Click on the **Fetch It** button.

FactHound will fetch the best sites for you!

Index